Hard Riddles

for
Smart Kids

DINGO
B O O K   C L U B

"Great Books Change Life"

Table of Contents

Introduction

It's been said that questions are signs of an active mind, which is crucial for children growing up to be intelligent, smart, and wise adults. Riddles are one of the best - and fun - ways of stimulating the mind so that it continues to become better and smarter.

In my first book Smart Riddles for Smart Kids, I gave you 400 fun and interactive riddles that you and your kids can enjoy. As promised in that book, I've compiled 400 harder riddles for you and your smart kids to enjoy answering! And as with the first book, the riddles here can provide very good mental stimulation for you and your kids, and help make your minds develop even more. I hope you enjoy them as much as the first book. Let's go!

Riddles 1 To 100

Question #1

Over the side of a ship hung a rope ladder that's 12 feet long. It has wooden rungs that are 12 inches apart and the lowest one is barely touching the water. The tide's going up by 4 inches every hour. How long before the 6 lowest rungs will be completely submerged in water?

Question #2

The brother of a very big boss passed away. How was the very big boss related to the brother that passed away?

Question #3

In a black-painted town where no street lights were working due to a very powerful storm that just blew by, a black dog was standing right smack in the middle of an intersection. A truck with no working headlights was speeding towards the intersection and the dog, but the driver was able to see the dog and was able to hit the brakes. How was the driver able to clearly see the dog?

Question #4

Jerry's a butcher who stands about 6 feet 3 inches and has a 50-inch waistline. What does he weigh?

Question #5

All but 8 of a farmer's 15 pigs died as a result of swine flu. How many pigs did the farmer have left?

Question #6

Before going inside the house, the farmer tied a 50-foot long rope on his horse's neck. 80 feet away from the horse was a bale of hay. When the farmer returned 2 hours after, he found his horse eating the bale of hay. How was the horse able to do it?

Question #7

If the yellow house is on your right and the black house is on your left, where is the white house located?

Question #8

A kitten who drinks a lot of lemonade is called what?

Question #9

Pedro, Berto, and Mamerto are kids living in the Caribbean. One day, they decided to race to the top of a very tall mango tree, where the first kid to reach the lemon on top will be crowned King of the Tree. Who do you think will win?

Question #10

A boy throws a baseball as hard as he can and yet, it returns to him no matter how hard he throws it away. Why?

Question #11

A clown at a children's party offered to give any kid who can keep his head underwater for more than 5 minutes without coming up, a prize money of $20. Ben, who is just 6 years old, volunteered and won the $20. How did he do it?

Question #12

To a clerk sitting behind a counter, Mark handed a book for scanning. The clerk said it would be $5.00 and after paying, Mark left the book. How come the clerk never called him to come back for the scanned book?

Question #13

At the center of a really big lake, a man was a prisoner. Unfortunately for the man, the lake was too large to swim to shore and there were no fences or bridges to walk on or climb. But still, the man was able to escape without any particular piece of equipment or a boat. How?

Question #14

Bronson was driving down his block when he saw 3 doors in front of him: a pink, a blue, and a green door. Which should he open first?

Question #15

Driving on his way to an appointment for which he was already running late, Michael turned a corner very quickly to the point where only 2 wheels were touching the ground. A cop sees that, but only gives him a nod and didn't bother to flag him down. Why?

Question #16

Jimmy lives on the 15th floor of his apartment building. Every day going to work, he takes the elevator going down. But when he comes home, he takes the stairs going back up to his apartment. Why does he do this?

Question #17

When Mister Robinson enters a restaurant he hasn't eaten in, the waiter immediately greets him "Good morning, General!" why did the waiter greet him that way?

Question #18

Jeffrey was about to buy a 2500 dollar car and he took it home without having to pay a dime? How was he able to do it?

Question #19

Michael was performing the duties of his job when he tore a hole in his suit. In merely 3 minutes, he died. Why?

Question #20

A motorcycle drove to a city and on the way, met 1,913 cars. How many vehicles were on their way to the village?

Question #21

Gertrude was a mute lady who walked into a convenience store. She signals to the store person that she wants to buy a can of Coke. After her, Billy the blind musician walks in, also looking to buy a can of Coke. How did he signal it to the store person?

Question #22

At a local hardware store, a gardener and a plumber were standing in line. One of them was the mother to the other person's daughter. How is this possible?

Question #23

On the top of a barn's roof, Jeffrey's rooster laid an egg. In which direction did the egg roll?

Question #24

How many sand piles would a child playing on the beach have if he has 3 small piles in one place and 4 large ones in another, and he put them all together?

Question #25

A substitute teacher saw that on the list of students enrolled in her class, one particular surname appeared. Curious, she inquired of the students if they all have the same birthdays, parents, and address - and all of them answered "yes" to all the questions. How can this be possible if they're not twins?

Question #26

A plane flying to Bermuda crashed. Where did the authorities bury the survivors?

Question #27

How can a man who shoots his best friend, submerges him for 5 minutes underwater, and hangs him go out with the same best friend 3 hours later to play basketball?

Question #28

Seeing a fly in her tea, a woman was flabbergasted! She asked the waiter to replace it with fresh, newly brewed tea, which the waiter did very quickly. After getting the new tea, the woman scolded the waiter saying it was the same tea. How could she have known it was the same tea?

Question #29

Mitchell's dad had 3 sons. The first was named Uno and the second one was named Dos. What was the name of the 3rd son?

Question #30

Prior to Mt. Everest's discovery, what was the tallest mountain?

Question #31

As shallow as a cup and small as a biscuit, even the biggest lakes and rivers can't fill it. What is this?

Question #32

Margaret has her own pet store and one of the animals she sells are canaries. If she puts just one canary in a cage, she'll have 1 canary without a cage. If she puts 2 in a cage, she'll have 1 cage without a canary. How many canaries and cages does Margaret have?

Question #33

How do you read this correctly: Days Between Days.

Question #34

I have a son who is exactly 1/5 of my age. I'll be exactly double his age after 21 years. My spouse is older than our daughter by 7 times and she'll be thrice as old as our daughter after 8 years. How old are our children now?

Question #35

Bridget's mom has 4 daughters: The first 3 are Eenie, Minnie, and Maynee. Who's the fourth?

Question #36
How many words are in this book you're reading?

Question #37
In an empty backpack, how many shirts can you put in?

Question #38
How many thirds are there in a year?

Question #39
Where in the world does the daughter come before the father?

Question #40
What's at the center of the earth?

Question #41

Spell the number 80 with just 2 letters.

Question #42

Can an adult elephant lift you with just one hand?

Question #43

What other countries have a 4th of July?

Question #44

How many sides does a circle have?

Question #45

Minho bikes every day across the border between Mexico and the United States with nothing but a small backpack. Yet, border patrols believe he's smuggling stuff across. But despite thoroughly frisking and searching Minho and his small bag, they can't find what it is he's smuggling. Do you know what Minho's smuggling across the border?

Question #46

The land mass of Italy looks like a boot. In what direction does the boot's toe face?

Question #47

Between the sparrow, ostrich, eagle, gull, and finch, which bird doesn't belong?

Question #48

Four friends - Reese, Debbie, Mike, and Bertha - ran across the yard in a tightly contested race. Debbie was behind Mike the same number of places as Bertha was ahead of Reese. Mike wasn't in first place and Reese wasn't in second. What were their placings?

Question #49

At the start of all ends and at the ends of each and every place, I am there. Even from the beginning of eternity and the end of time, I'm there. What am I?

Question #50

Bite she can't though she has teeth, and hold she can't though hands possess. Feet of hers aren't warm but cold, and she can't see though eyes her sockets hold. What is she?

Question #51

He who has married so many ladies is himself a single person. Who is he?

Question #52

How can New York ever be right beside North Carolina?

Question #53

How can a raw egg fall on a cement floor without breaking it?

Question #54

How is it that each and every one of your cousins have a common uncle that's not your uncle also?

Question #55

How can you cross a field of grass but only move 2 feet?

Question #56

How was Darth Vader able to predict what Luke Skywalker would be getting for the holidays?

Question #57

How can you keep the breath of your Christmas trees perpetually fresh?

Question #58

What's the right way to say the name of Kentucky's capital: Loo-iss-ville or Loo-ee-ville?

Question #59

How far can you drive your truck into an open field?

Question #60

How can you cut nails thrice daily and still have your nails grow long?

Question #61

How many birthdays will you have in your lifetime?

Question #62

How many pairs of animals did Moses bring into the ark before the great flood?

Question #63

From a whole loaf of white bread, how many slices can you cut?

Question #64

How many 4-inch pieces of rope are in a dozen?

Question #65

How many times can you subtract 5 from 50?

Question #66

How many marbles were there in an empty box that measures 20 inches long by 10 inches wide and 5 inches deep?

Question #67

What's the maximum you should pay to buy a skunk?

Question #68

How can you walk on water for real?

Question #69

It sleeps with shoes and it sleeps while standing. What is it?

Question #70

It has a horn and gives milk and yet, it isn't a cow. What is it?

Question #71

Loud am I because of my big mouth and despite involving myself in other people's dirt, I never gossip. What am I?

Question #72

I can't see yet I have a big eye. Though I have no limbs I outrun the fastest people alive. What Am I?

Question #73

I can't fly though 4 wings have I. Never have I laughed, and never have I cried. Yet, I toil away with little sound, always being in the same place where found. What am I?

Question #74

I have hands that wave but never for goodbyes. You'll always be cool when to you I say HI. What am I?

Question #75

I have a strong back, but I don't work. I have legs but never walk. I have arms, but never reach. I have a seat, yet I don't sit down. What am I?

Question #76

It's a word that becomes fewer when you add 2 more letters. What is it?

Question #77

My house is small, in it I'm alone. Doors and windows it has not and for me to go out, it's walls I must crack. Who am I?

Question #78

Before the sun I pass, but shadow not I have. What am I?

Question #79

I'm just a collection of connected holes, but I'm flexible compared to a pole and as strong as steel. What am I?

Question #80

You can't see me because I'm so fast, I will only stop when you die, and all people see straight through me. What am I?

Question #81

A doctor tells Jordan to take 3 tablets after every half hour. How long did it take Jordan to down all 3 pills?

Question #82

An eagle comes flying into New York's Empire State Building. From where did it come from originally?

Question #83

An electric-powered car is moving northward at 50 miles per hour and a southeastern wind is blowing against it at 20 miles per hour. In which direction will the car's smoke drift?

Question #84

To dig five holes in one hour, it takes 7 men. To dig half a hole, how many hours will one man need?

Question #85

It took 20 hours for 50 men to erect a wall that's 50 feet long and 30 feet high. If 25 men were to build it, how many hours would it take?

Question #86

What is it that you can surely count on regardless of what happens in your life?

Question #87

There were 100 pieces of chocolate candy on the table. You took 30 pieces. How many do you have?

Question #88

How many times can you add 20 to the number 100?

Question #89

Why do sharks prefer to swim in salt water only?

Question #90

If you combine a pig and a chicken, what'll you get?

Question #91

If you perform 20 pushups daily, 30 squats daily, and 100 sit-ups every day, what would be your biggest organ?

Question #92

If Dory and Dumbo got married and had twins, what would their children be?

Question #93

How can you make your left shoe bigger without touching or moving it?

Question #94

What happens to a black sports car that plunges off a cliff and into the Red Sea in Israel?

Question #95

You are being chased by rabid wolves and the road you're running on reaches a trident with 3 routes you can take to escape. The first route is a trail riddled with land mines. The second route is a road littered with ultra-fast and strong zombies like those from World War Z and Train to Busan. The last route is a stream filled with Piranhas that haven't eaten in 20 years. Which route is the safest?

Question #96

If you etch yours and your sweetheart's names on the bark of a tree at about 5 feet from the ground, how high would your names on the bark be after 5 years if the baby tree grows by about 10 inches every year?

Question #97

You have 10 pieces of candy and lose 3 of them due to being forgetful. How many have you left?

Question #98

You enter a dark room with a TV, a refrigerator, a microwave oven, and an air-conditioning unit. What would you switch on first?

Question #99

If you put your music playing device in the refrigerator, what will you get?

Question #100

If you overtook the person who was in 10th place in an ultramarathon, what place would you be in now?

Riddles 101 To 200

Question #101

You're 10 meters away from the finish line and with every step you take, you move half the remaining distance to the finish line. When will you reach the finish line?

Question #102

Imagine you're a pilot flying a Boeing 747 jumbo jet across the Atlantic. The plane has 500 passengers on board, including the pilot. Of the 500 passengers, only 200 are male and the rest are female. Of the 200 male passengers, only 10 were older than 60 years old, 100 were younger than 10 years old, and the rest were between 10 and 60 years old. What's the gender and age of the pilot?

Question #103

In the city you live in, there are only 2 barbers: Mike and Geoff. Mike's hair is well maintained and looks really beautiful while that of Geoff's is cut very poorly. If you want to look good, which barber should you go to for a haircut?

Question #104

Where in the world is it legal for a man to marry the sister of his widow?

Question #105

Why is it impossible to shoot pictures of a person with a wooden leg?

Question #106

In the United States, up to 95% of all landline telephone numbers are listed, where 70% of listed numbers are businesses and the rest are residential. If you were to conduct a survey and sample 900 numbers using the phone book, how many can you reasonably expect to be unlisted?

Question #107

How much dirt would you need for an open grave?

Question #108

It always goes up and down for a ride and it's also the present and past tense of another word. What is it?

Question #109

People eat the least during this month. What month is this?

Question #110

It receives its assignment the night before and if it completes it, people get mad at it. What is it?

Question #111

It can never flee even if it runs. It can never see even if it's watched. Too much of it breeds boredom, but lack of it brings fear. What is it?

Question #112

It begins as black, and it turns red when used. Once it's done, it becomes white. What is it?

Question #113

It's always in between the sky and the earth, but always at such a far distance, and it moves further away the more one tries to get closer to it. What is it?

Question #114

Despite existing for more than a million years, it never becomes older than 1 month. What is it?

Question #115

It's killed by direct light, but indirect light creates it. What is it?

Question #116

Jeremy's uncle only had 4 nephews. The first three were named June, July, and August. Who was the 4th nephew?

Question #117

As Morgan was driving along a highway, he encounters a detour. What did he do?

Question #118

James has an aquarium with 5 small and 20 big fishes. Unfortunately, 2 small and 10 big fishes died. How many fishes remained in the water?

Question #119

Mr. and Mrs. Smith have 9 kids. Half of them are girls. How is that possible?

Question #120

Bees are hovering flowers on a pond. If every bee lands on a flower such that one bee doesn't get a flower, and when 2 bees share a flower one flower doesn't have a bee, how many flowers and bees are there in that pond?

Question #121

When was the last time that New Year Day came before Christmas Day?

Question #122

It's always on the move, though silently it does so. While it neither walks nor trots, anywhere's cool where it is not. What is it?

Question #123

Of all the tires of your car, which one doesn't turn right?

Question #124

Two boys play 7 games of tennis. Each boy wins the same number of games, but there are no games that ended in a tie. How did it happen?

Question #125

On normal days, how much milk can a full-grown cow drink?

Question #126

For a house being made completely of bricks, how many bricks are needed to finish the house?

Question #127

You were on your way to Oracle Arena to watch the Golden State Warriors thrash the Phoenix Suns. On the way, you met "hi" to 15 childhood friends, 20 church mates, and 50 acquaintances. How many people were on their way to the Oracle Arena?

Question #128

A family of 3 cats - Momma, Poppa, and Kid cat - were crossing the street at midnight. From out of nowhere, a Harley Davidson motorcycle came speeding. Luckily, the Poppa was alert enough to stop Momma and Kid cats. As a result, no one got hurt. Momma cat was so agitated she said something to Poppa cat. What did she say?

Question #129

If a criminal was condemned to die for the crime he committed and the King asked him how he'd like to die, what should the criminal answer so he won't be executed but instead be let go?

Question #130

A man once turned off all the lights before going to sleep at night. The next morning, he was shocked to see so many dead people. What happened?

Question #131

In this sentence, one word is spelled incorrectly. What word is that?

Question #132

Mark and Mike are twins. On a specific year, Mark celebrated his birthday 2 days before Mike's. How'd that happen?

Question #133

What's the first thing that comes to mind: What do you put inside a toaster?

Question #134

Which scenario will you most probably survive: A hungry lion attacking you or a tiger?

Question #135

In a bedroom, both Jim and Janice were found dead. There was water and some shattered glass on the floor in the room where they were found. Looking around the room, you can only find a bed and a shelf. The house - where the room is located - is situated in a very remote area near the railroad tracks. What caused the death of the two?

Question #136

I'm as deep as a well yet round as a button. For me to talk, my tail you must pull. What am I?

Question #137

Veterinarians discovered that when it comes to cats, one side has more hair than the others. Which side is that?

Question #138

You can take away my first second third and all of my letters and still I will not change. What am I?

Question #139

If I asked you if your shirt had holes and you said no, would that be the right answer?

Question #140

There were 20 copycats riding at the back of a pickup truck. One of them jumps off the truck. How many were left?

Question #141

"My lawyer happens to be my brother", the accountant said while being questioned in a court trial. But the lawyer intern testified that he has no brother. Which of the two was lying?

Question #142

If the peacock is a type of bird that does not produce any eggs, then where in the world do peacock chicks come from?

Question #143

Margaret traveled to Transylvania to teach Count Dracula not to drin

k blood from humans. How many T's were in that?

Question #144

On the branches of a particular tree sat 50 crows. One of them was captured by a snake. How many were left?

Question #145

There were 20 bananas in a basket. There were 20 children in the room. If each child got one banana, how come there's one banana left in the basket?

Question #146

There were a hundred gold fishes in a big aquarium. 1/4 of them, or 25 gold fishes, drowned. How many were left?

Question #147

If you have a total of 55 cents made up of two coins and one of them isn't a nickel, what are those two coins?

Question #148

If you were asked to accurately predict the score of any ball game right before it starts, whether it's a basketball, baseball, or football game, what can you say that will always be correct?

Question #149

This is a very exciting sport we're both the audience and the players have no idea of the scores until it's over. What is this sport?

Question #150

When a deadly fire broke out in a factory, each and every single person suffered serious injuries except for 2 people. How did that happen?

Question #151

They can either bring life or death, they can either be food or poison - it's really up to you which of those they will be. What are they?

Question #152

How do you say I would love to swim in Martian language?

Question #153

During every inning of a baseball game, how many outs are needed for it to be over?

Question #154

It never walks but it always runs, it never talks but it has a mouth, it has a bed but never sleeps, it has a head but never weeps. What is it?

Question #155

In the hospital, the three doctors that attended to Michael in the emergency room all said Michael was their brother. But when asked, Michael claimed he had no brothers. Was Michael or the three doctors lying?

Question #156

One evening, 5 robbers forced their way into a store, but upon leaving they completely changed. Despite that, however, they went to another store and robbed it completely. How did that happen?

Question #157

Michael left Boston to go to Chicago, driving at an average speed of 50 miles per hour. Larry on the other hand left Chicago driving to Boston at an average speed of 60 miles per hour. When they met each other along the way, which of them was farther from Boston - Michael or Larry?

Question #158

In a car going to Walmart, there were two mothers and two daughters. But when the car got to Walmart, only 3 people got out. Why?

Question #159

In what educational material does it say that the universe came after man?

Question #160

Using nothing else but a single hand, how many times can you fold a letter-sized sheet of white paper?

Question #161

If you trample on their dead, they grumble and mutter, but if you travel on their living, you won't hear a chatter. What are they?

Question #162

Some months of the year have 30 days and others have 31 days. How many months have 28 days?

Question #163

What is it that ends life?

Question #164

Why do the strongest people in the world love Saturdays and Sundays?

Question #165

What kind of building has the most number of stories?

Question #166

What is something that can swallow you which you can prevent by swallowing it instead?

Question #167

It stings the mouth and can burn the eyes. And yet, you can consume it. What is it?

Question #168

Even without moving from its place, it can go up and down. What is it?

Question #169

It's something that you can put inside a big box that can make it lighter. What is it?

Question #170

The night before Christmas, what did Adam say?

Question #171

Whenever the toys that he made and gave showed attitude problems, what does Santa say?

Question #172

When Santa gave a bald man a comb for his Christmas gift, what did the bald man say?

Question #173

When ice screams, what do bananas do?

Question #174

When dining in restaurants, what do sea monsters love to order?

Question #175

During Thanksgiving, what do vampires pour on their turkeys?

Question #176

What do volcanoes infatuated with each other tell each other?

Question #177

When somebody writes a song about cars, what do you call that song?

Question #178

If you see a zipper on a banana, what do you call it?

Question #179

If a person doesn't have all fingers in his right hand, what do you call him?

Question #180

If your mother in law has a child, what do you call that child's father in law?

Question #181

If you combine the Christmas tree with an apple, what do you get?

Question #182

If you combine a tiger with a parrot, what do you have?

Question #183

If you fuse Albert Einstein with SpongeBob Squarepants, what do you get?

Question #184

What is the one thing in December that other months can never have?

Question #185

What do you brush your teeth with, sleep on, and sit on?

Question #186

A cow signs up to go to outer space. Once outside the Earth's atmosphere and in outer space, what does a cow say?

Question #187

This is another thing that despite staying put in its place, goes up and down. What is it?

Question #188

If you eat all of your house's Christmas decorations, what sickness do you get?

Question #189

During an earthquake, what happens to cows?

Question #190

During the summer, what happens to your pet dogs?

Question #191

It has two feet - 1 each per side - and another in the middle. What is it?

Question #192

Vampires hate taking tests except for this one. What is this test?

Question #193

This is something that is heavy at first, but becomes light the moment you reverse it. What is it?

Question #194

This is something where taking from the whole leaves some leftover. What is it?

Question #195

What is Dwayne "The Rock" Johnson's second name?

Question #196

What is at the center of the sun?

Question #197

What makes a farmer watching his cattle different from a schoolboy studying his lessons?

Question #198

Do you know the alphabet? What is the first letter of the alphabet?

Question #199

All cans need a can opener to be useful except this one. What is this can?

Question #200

What do you call a flying monkey?

Riddles 201 To 300

Question #201

All rooms typically have a door or a window except for this one. What kind of room doesn't have a door or a window?

Question #202

This kind of running is the same as walking. What is this kind of running?

Question #203

It's something that resembles half an apple. What is it?

Question #204

No matter how heavy it rains, it stays just as wet. What is it?

Question #205

It's a number that has 3 digits. The digit that corresponds to tens is 5 times more than the digit that corresponds to the ones. Its hundreds digit is eight times lower than the digit for the tens. What number is it?

Question #206

This part of the turkey contains the most number of feathers. What part is this?

Question #207

You can ask this question to a person all day long, all month long, and all year long and you will hardly ever get the same answers. What is this question?

Question #208

What is the one question that you will never be able to answer personally?

Question #209

What is one question that you will always answer with a "yes"?

Question #210

It's a 6 letter word that contains letters in perfect alphabetical order?

Question #211

It smelled bad when it was alive, but when it was dead, it smelled really good. What is it?

Question #212

It starts in New York and ends in Dublin. Then it starts in Nigeria and finishes in Spain. What is it?

Question #213

It stays in place even when it goes off? What is it?

Question #214

It's a combination of words that has the most letters ever. What is this combination?

Question #215

Back in 1980, what was the president's name?

Question #216

What would a traffic light shout to your car as you're driving it?

Question #217

What goes up and down, up and down and is red and white all over?

Question #218

Why is the Christmas alphabet so unique?

Question #219

What is the one thing that both your teeth and your plants have in common?

Question #220

It's black and white, black and white, and black and white. What is it?

Question #221

Where can you find adding the number 2 to the number 11 resulting in the number 1?

Question #222

Where on earth does Thanksgiving follow Christmas?

Question #223

Point it up, it's bright. Point it down, it's no longer bright. What is it?

Question #224

When are you encouraged to go when red and stop when green?

Question #225

Every time Santa Claus leaves the North Pole on Christmas Eve to bring gifts to children all over the world, in what direction does he go?

Question #226

Where do the largest and most delicious potatoes grow?

Question #227

Which of the two clocks works better: The one that doesn't work at all or the one that loses one minute every day?

Question #228

Which is heavier: A ton of steel or 2 tons of cotton?

Question #229

Between these two statements, which is correct: "All carrot are green" or "All carrots are greens"?

Question #230

Which of the two triangles has a bigger area: Triangle A whose sides measure 500, 400, and 300 millimeters, or Triangle B whose side's measure 700, 400, 300 millimeters?

Question #231

It's not only children who get Christmas gifts - dogs get them too! Who gives Christmas gifts to dogs?

Question #232

On Thanksgiving, it's the only one that never gets hungry. What is this?

Question #233

When this person moves, he can remain seated. Who is this person?

Question #234

There was another reindeer mentioned in the Christmas song Rudolph The Red-Nosed Reindeer. Who was that reindeer?

Question #235

There are three people in the Bigger family: Mr. Bigger, Mrs. Bigger, and their baby. Who among them was the biggest?

Question #236

It's maker doesn't tell. It's takers do not know. And those who know don't want it. What is it?

Question #237

Why are 2018 dollar bills worth more than 2017 dollar bills?

Question #238

A banana checked with a doctor the other day. Why did it do so?

Question #239

A bee once approached a flower and asked a question. What question was that?

Question #240

A box of sand weighs 10 pounds. Without taking anything out of it, what can you add to the box to make it weigh less than 10 pounds?

Question #241

A brunette, a blond, and a redhead all jump off the cliff and hit the waters. Who hit the waters last?

Question #242

A bus driver didn't stop at a stop light, turned right at a left-turn-only street, and enters a one-way street and yet, the cops didn't flag him. Why?

Question #243

A cake loves playing baseball. Why?

Question #244

A caterpillar takes so long to leave it's house. Why?

Question #245

A chocolate chip cookie consulted with a doctor. Why?

Question #246

A man bets another man. He said "I'll write on paper whatever you're thinking even if you don't say a word!" The man won the bet. How'd he do it?

Question #247

Adam has only one, eve has 2, and everybody has 2 as well. What is it?

Question #248

Among my friends I'm the thinnest. I'm in the Philippines but never in Japan. What am I?

Question #249

Around a field it goes, and yet it never ever moves. What is it?

Question #250

Aside from a snake, what can move without having any feet?

Question #251

At parties, it's the only thing that needs to be broken. What is it?

Question #252

At the center of the universe they lie. What are they?

Question #253

At times I flow, at times I fall. And when I come, you cover all. What am I?

Question #254

Badder than the devil, bigger than God, the poor have me and the rich can't have me. Eating me means death. What am I?

Question #255

Ben and Jerry went on a trip where if they look towards the north, they see the sun and when they look towards the south, all they see are stars and darkness. Where did they go?

Question #256

Bikes aren't known for being able to stand up on their own. Why?

Question #257

Despite being light and being able to float on water, no man in his hand can ever carry her? What is it?

Question #258

Despite being mostly in a shade, it brightens up your surroundings. What is it?

Question #259

Despite killing hundreds of people, why wasn't Catrina sentenced to jail?

Question #260

Dwayne "The Rock" Johnson has one and Zendaya has none. What is it?

Question #261

Eskimos are known to never hunt penguins, even if it means starving to death. Why?

Question #262

Every game, our team is on field or court. And despite not scoring a single point, our team never loses. Why?

Question #263

Everybody does this first thing in the morning. What is it?

Question #264

Fortune tellers have a favorite tree that they use to tell people's fortunes. What tree is this?

Question #265

How can 20 men not get wet under just 1 umbrella?

Question #266

How can a father lose more than 100 pounds in just 1 day?

Question #267

How can you be armed even without weapons?

Question #268

How do dogs and cats stop a video or music player?

Question #269

How will you be able to break inside a house without having to smash the windows or kick the doors open?

Question #270

How's a teacher and a train different?

Question #271

I am nothing when people know me and am something when people don't know me. What am I?

Question #272

I can be tall when standing, but I'm definitely more when sitting. What am I?

Question #273

I can go side to side but never up and down. What am I?

Question #274

I can run at times, but never walk. And behind me not far away are thoughts. What am I?

Question #275

I cover things up only to make them more obvious. What am I?

Question #276

I don't stop working even if you break me. I may be snared if you touch me. And if you lose me, nothing else matters. What am I?

Question #277

I have a hard heart but sweet and soft is my flesh. What am I?

Question #278

I make noises sometimes, but often times I don't. I never end and people also wear me. What am I?

Question #279

I may be water's sons, but when I return to it, I'm dead. What am I?

Question #280

I see not yet for me bright is the dark. What am I?

Question #281

I was born in 1980 but as of 2017, I'm just 20 years old. How'd that happen?

Question #282

I'm a pet, but immovable am I on the floor while the whole family steps on me more and more. What am I?

Question #283

I'm not a hole but the more you take from me, the bigger I become. What am I?

Question #284

I'm soft but hard, solid yet liquid, clear yet with color. What am I?

Question #285

I'm square and I'm blue. What am I?

Question #286

I'm the only number that when added to and multiplied by myself, the same answer is obtained. What number am I?

Question #287

If a Nazi has colds and a runny nose, what do you call it?

Question #288

If an octopus graduated from med school and is taking up residence in a hospital, what is it called?

Question #289

If Captain Morgan had a ship, what is its name?

Question #290

If cars can swim, where would they do it?

Question #291

If fishes want to get high, what do they smoke?

Question #292

If for some reason you find yourself trapped inside a car with a bat, what should you do?

Question #293

If I ask you to spell the word "candy" with just 2 letters, how'd you do it?

Question #294

If I asked you to jump from a 50 story building and survive without any injuries, how'd you do it?

Question #295

If the chicken isn't able to cross the road successfully, what is it called?

Question #296

If you are halfway there and halfway gone, where are you?

Question #297

If you get bitten by a vampire during winter, what will you get?

Question #298

If you lick an envelope, what does it say?

Question #299

If you put 2 quarters inside your ears, what would you hear?

Question #300

Where do fishes save their hard-earned money?

Riddles 301 To 400

Question #301

If your dog is tied to a 20-foot leash, how can it reach a bone that's 5 feet away?

Question #302

In a cafeteria, the clock runs very slow. Why's that so?

Question #303

In every corner, there's one and in every room, there's 2. What is it?

Question #304

In front of you I am, but see me clearly you can't. What am I?

Question #305

In the middle of the night, you were abruptly woken up to find that your walls were peeling, your roof and ceiling were smoking, and the water in your house was boiling. Which of these should you address first?

Question #306

Is this sentence false: true or false?

Question #307

It becomes wetter the more it dries. What is it?

Question #308

Imagine you're in a plane that's about to crash onto Mt. Everest. The pilot's dead and you're the only one alive in the plane. What should you do to survive?

Question #309

It catches flies and has 18 legs. What is it?

Question #310

It claims to have 25 toes, is as tall as an electric post, and wasn't born to a father and mother. What is it?

Question #311

It has 1 eye and a tail. When it passes through something, the edge of its tail gets trapped. What is it?

Question #312

It has 2 heads yet one body. It runs faster the stiller it stands. What is it?

Question #313

It has 2 heads, 1 tail, 4 eyes, and 6 legs. What creature is this?

Question #314

It has a tail, 4 legs, a tail, and goes "oooom, ooooom!" What is it?

Question #315

It has no body and yet it has ears. It has no mouth and yet it can speak. What is it?

Question #316

It has pointed fangs that wait to be used on bloodless victims, forever joining them in just one bite. What is it?

Question #317

It passes through glass, and yet it doesn't break it. What is it?

Question #318

It touches only one person, but binds two. What is it?

Question #319

It's a little man with a staff in his hand, a red coat, and stone-filled throat. Who is he?

Question #320

It weighs exactly 2,000 pounds. What is it?

Question #321

It's all over the world and the galaxy and yet, it's as thin as paper. What is it?

Question #322

It's always on track, but never makes it. What is it?

Question #323

It's an animal who you can transform into a bigger one simply by removing one letter from its name. What animal is this?

Question #324

It's been recently discovered that animals in Africa don't like playing games together. Why?

Question #325

It's green and turns red after going 100 miles-per-hour. What is it?

Question #326

It's not famous, but has lots of fans. What is it?

Question #327

It's stronger than many men and yet, it can't stand on its own. What is it?

Question #328

It's the only nut that has no shell. What is it?

Question #329

James went into a store and bought something expensive. He gave that thing to a random person, who gave it back to him after a short while. What is it that James bought in the store?

Question #330

Jamie was reading when his brother turned the lights off. Jamie just continued reading in the dark. How was this possible?

Question #331

Jane was born in 1948 and in 1979, she gave birth to Darwin. In 2006, her son Darwin was older than her! How'd that happen?

Question #332

Jim's a fisherman who stands 6 feet 5 inches. He's also very fat. What does he weigh?

Question #333

Like a beautiful river I flow, but once you drink me, away your life will go. What am I?

Question #334

Like an apple, it's round. Like a cup it's deep. But all the men in the world combined can't pull it up. What is it?

Question #335

Marge didn't have a good relationship with her dad and never will. The mother never encouraged her to have a better relationship with him either. Why?

Question #336

Micah tells you that everything she tells you is a lie. Is she right or wrong?

Question #337

Mike and Marv made a bet. If Mike was able to ask a question that Marv can't answer, then Marv would give Mike $5 but if Marv was able to do the same to Mike, he'd get $20 from Mike. Mike had access to the Internet so he could've Googled practically any question that Marv could ask, but at the end of the bet, Marv got $20. How'd that happen?

Question #338

My lightning only comes after my thunder. My rain only follows my thunder and it scorches all that it touches. What am I?

Question #339

My mom gave birth to a baby, but it's neither my brother nor sister. Who is the baby?

Question #340

My mom and dad had kids on the same year and day, but they weren't twins. How'd that happen?

Question #341

On a white hill were 30 horses. These horses first clamp, then stamp, and finally stand still. What are they?

Question #342

On stage at a stand-up comedy place, Casper the friendly ghost bombed with really corny jokes. What did the crowd shout at him?

Question #343

One night, a man and woman went to the pier to see if they can ride a boat. The only available boat had a big sign that says "only 2 people on board so it won't sink". They hopped on the boat and still it sank. Why?

Question #344

Pinocchio always wins spelling bees and always scores very high on his tests in school. Why?

Question #345

Six is very scared of running into seven. Why?

Question #346

The force of strong men can't break through, but with a light touch I can do. Many would be out on the streets, if in their hands I would never be. What am I?

Question #347

The king sits on gold. Who sits on top of silver?

Question #348

The start of awesomeness I am, and conclude every comma do I. Inside a stomach I stay so therefore, what am I?

Question #349

There was a family of 3 wanting to cross the river on a raft. The raft can only carry a maximum weight of 200 pounds. The father weighs 200 pounds, the mother weighs 100 pounds, and the son weighs 100 pounds too. How can they all cross the river using the raft?

Question #350

These are tables without legs. What are they?

Question #351

Thirty heads went under the water and when they went back up, there were 34 heads. How'd that happen?

Question #352

This number sequence is an encrypted message: 29125.

Question #353

To carry lots of stuff, what does an elephant use?

Question #354

Two battleships squared off in the Pacific Ocean, firing a torpedo at each other. The radar showed that the torpedoes disappeared despite no other retaliation from either battleship or no other objects entering the combat or radar zone. What happened to the torpedoes?

Question #355

Two brothers are we, our skin shades are opposites completely. I come from the sea and not my brother, but despite the contrast, we're great together. What are we?

Question #356

Vampires are known to be easily tricked or conned. Why is that so?

Question #357

We all drink water. Why?

Question #358

We see it every day, the President hardly does, and God can never find it. What is it?

Question #359

What do you call pigs' favorite martial arts move?

Question #360

What do you call sweet treats that are clever?

Question #361

What do you call the country of fishes?

Question #362

What ends the universe?

Question #363

What's in between you and me?

Question #364

What is a find called?

Question #365

What is MCE, MCE, MCE?

Question #366

What is the official pet dog of Count Dracula?

Question #367

What is the one place where you're sure to find everything you need?

Question #368

What is the only word in the dictionary that's spelled properly?

Question #369

What makes here and there different?

Question #370

What river in the world doesn't flow?

Question #371

What will you always see in middle of the night?

Question #372

What word is spelled backwards?

Question #373

What's the easiest way to catch fish?

Question #374

What's the right way to read this: YY 4ME YY UR?

Question #375

When a duck approaches the store cashier and is asked how it'll pay, what does it always say?

Question #376

When gorilla kids go to school for the first time, what do they learn first?

Question #377

When I was young I was tall, now that I'm old I am short. Alive I do glow, but a breath of life is my staunchest foe. What am I?

Question #378

When I'm bad, I'm good but when I'm asleep, I'm hurt. What am I?

Question #379

When it comes to the English language, only a couple of words end in "gry". One is "angry". The second word is "hungry". What's the third word in the English language?

Question #380

When it's on, it flies. When it's off, it floats. What is it?

Question #381

While you can never win this kind of a game, you will never lose it too. What game is this?

Question #382

Who first made gun powder?

Question #383

Why did Casper the Ghost skip the prom?

Question #384

Why did the cat run from the dog?

Question #385

Why did the chicken cross playground?

Question #386

Why do birds always fly south?

Question #387

With many words am I composed, and lots of information I give to all. What am I?

Question #388

You always see me 2 times a week, 1 time every year, and never every month. What am I?

Question #389

You can hold it and yet never get to touch it. What is it?

Question #390

You can surf any wave except for this one. What wave is this?

Question #391

You can't catch me, but you can hear me. What am I?

Question #392

You can't eat trees except for this one. What tree is this?

Question #393

You finally decide to paint your room blue and decided to apply 3 coats of paint. Of the 3 coats, which would go on the first coat?

Question #394

You got locked inside a sealed bathroom. Unfortunately, you broke the handles of a bathtub while trying to fill it up with water and now, you can't turn the water off. The water spills over from the tub and is now threatening to flood the whole room and drown you. What should you do to survive?

Question #395

You have a bucket painted in red. What's it called?

Question #396

You place your mug on a table such that it's facing south and you're facing north. On which side is your mug's handle facing?

Question #397

You went to bed at 9 pm and set the alarm for 10. How many hours of sleep will you get?

Question #398

You're flying a jumbo jet from Manila, Philippines to Los Angeles, California. The jet's average flying speed is 550 miles-per-hour. It's traveling in a straight northwestern direction. It stops over at the Hawaii airport before proceeding to Los Angeles. If there were 500 passengers on board, how old was the pilot?

Question #399

You drive to your parents' house on Tuesday, but leave 5 days later still on Tuesday. How'd you do it?

Question #400

It can't smile yet it has a face. What is it?

Answers

Answers 1-10

Answer #1: Forever because as the tide rises, so does the boat and the rope ladder hanging from it.

Answer #2: She was the sister.

Answer #3: It happened during day time.

Answer #4: Meat. He's a butcher, remember?

Answer #5: 8 because "all but 8 died".

Answer #6: While the horse was tied to the rope, the rope wasn't tied to anything on the other end.

Answer #7: In Washington DC.

Answer #8: A sourpuss

Answer #9: None, because lemons don't grown on mango trees.

Answer #10: It's because he threw it straight upward. Gravity ensures it'll return to him regardless of how strong he throws it upward.

Answers 11-20

Answer #11: He put a glass of water on top of his head, which literally put his head under water (albeit in a glass) and let it stay there for more than 5 minutes.

Answer #12: The clerk was the librarian and mark merely paid for the overdue fee.

Answer #13: He waited until winter when the lake water's frozen solid, which allowed him to walk on it to freedom.

Answer #14: His car door.

Answer #15: Michael was driving a motorcycle, which only has 2 wheels.

Answer #16: It's because he's too short to reach the 15th floor button of the elevator but he's tall enough to reach the ground floor button.

Answer #17: Because mister Robinson was wearing his military uniform that shows his rank.

Answer #18: Jeffrey was about to buy a 2500 dollar car and he took it home without having to pay a dime. How was he able to do it? He paid $2500 in check.

Answer #19: At that time, he was an astronaut doing a space walk outside the space shuttle in space.
Answer #20: One - the motorcycle

Answers 21-30

Answer #21: He asked for a can of coke because he may be blind, but he can talk.

Answer #22: They were a married couple, i.e., a husband and a wife.

Answer #23: Roosters don't lay eggs and as such, no rolling took place.

Answer #24: One big pile only.

Answer #25: They're triplets.

Answer #26: They didn't because the survivors were alive!

Answer #27: The man was a photographer who shot his friend's picture using an old-school camera that still used film. To develop the picture, it had to be dipped in water for 5 minutes and hung out to dry. She already added honey to the first tea and when she tasted the newly brewed tea, it was already sweet, meaning it was the same content.

Answer #28: She already put honey on the first cup of tea and when she tasted the second one, it was already sweet with honey despite not putting any yet.

Answer #29: Mitchell.

Answer #30: Everest. Being undiscovered didn't mean it wasn't the tallest mountain in the world.

Answers 31-40

Answer #31: A kitchen strainer.

Answer #32: 4 canaries and 3 cages.

Answer #33: In between days.

Answer #34: Our son is 7 and our daughter's just 4 years old.

Answer #35: Bridget.

Answer #36: Four (4): this, book, you're, reading.

Answer #37: Only one, after which it's no longer empty.

Answer #38: Twelve, one for every month, e.g., January 3rd, February 3rd, etc.

Answer #39: Dictionary, letter d comes before letter f.

Answer #40: The letter r.

Answers 41-50

Answer #41: A and t.

Answer #42: No, they don't have hands.

Answer #43: All of them.

Answer #44: Two - the inside and the outside.

Answer #45: Bikes.

Answer #46: Forward, of course. No toe faces backward, right?

Answer #47: The ostrich because it's the only one that can't fly.

Answer #48: Bertha, Mike, Reese, and Debbie in 1st, 2nd, 3rd, and 4th places, respectively.

Answer #49: The letter "e".

Answer #50: A doll.

Answers 51-60

Answer #51: A catholic priest.

Answer #52: When it's on an alphabetically arranged list of states.

Answer #53: The egg won't break the floor because the floor's harder than the egg.

Answer #54: The uncle is your dad.

Answer #55: Simple, you only have 2 feet to move as you walk.

Answer #56: He felt his presents (presence).

Answer #57: With orna-mints.

Answer #58: Both are wrong because the real capital of Kentucky is Frankfort.

Answer #59: Only halfway because beyond that, you're already driving out of it.

Answer #60: You're a manicurist who cuts other people's nails at the salon.

Answers 61-70

Answer #61: Only one. All your other birthdays are just anniversaries of your birthday.

Answer #62: None. It was Noah who built the ark.

Answer #63: Only one because the bread's no longer whole after the first slice. Thus, your succeeding slices will be from a loaf of bread that's no longer whole.

Answer #64: 12, although I suspect that you initially thought 3.

Answer #65: Just once because the next time you do, it'd be from the number 45.

Answer #66: None. The box is empty, remember?

Answer #67: One cent (scent) only.

Answer #68: Let it freeze so you can walk over it.

Answer #69: A horse.

Answer #70: A milk truck.

Answers 71-80

Answer #71: A vacuum cleaner.

Answer #72: I am a hurricane.

Answer #73: A windmill.

Answer #74: An electric fan.

Answer #75: An armchair.

Answer #76: The word "few".

Answer #77: A chick in an egg.

Answer #78: The wind.

Answer #79: A steel chain.

Answer #80: A blink of an eye.

Answers 81-90

Answer #81: One hour only. It's because Jordan took the 1st pill immediately after the doctor told him to, the 2nd after 30 minutes, and the 3rd after an hour.

Answer #82: From an egg.

Answer #83: None, because electric cars don't produce smoke.

Answer #84: None. It's impossible to dig just half a hole. All holes are whole.

Answer #85: None. The 25 men can't build what was already built.

Answer #86: Your fingers.

Answer #87: 30 - that's how many you took from the table.

Answer #88: Only once because the next time you do, it'll be to the number 120.

Answer #89: Pepper makes them sneeze.

Answer #90: Bacon and eggs!

Answers 91-100

Answer #91: Your skin.

Answer #92: A pair of swimming trunks.

Answer #93: Put a smaller shoe beside it so it would become the "bigger" shoe.

Answer #94: It becomes a wet, black sports car.

Answer #95: The last route because piranhas that haven't eaten in 20 years would already be dead ones.

Answer #96: 5 feet because it wouldn't move as trees grow at the top only.

Answer #97: Only 3 because you left (i.e., forgot to bring or lost) 3 pieces and brought with you the remaining 7 pieces.

Answer #98: The lights.

Answer #99: Cool music!

Answer #100: Tenth.

Answers 101-110

Answer #101: Never because no matter how small the remaining distance gets, you'll only be moving forward by half of it.

Answer #102: Your gender and age, because you're the pilot in this situation, remember?

Answer #103: Geoff, because given only he and Mike are the barbers in town, it means his ugly hair was cut by Mike and Mike's beautiful looking hair was cut by Geoff.

Answer #104: Nowhere. How can a dead man - he has to be dead to have a widow - legally marry anyone for that matter?

Answer #105: Because you can't use any wooden object to take pictures. You can only with a camera.

Answer #106: None. Unlisted numbers wouldn't appear in a listing such as a phone book.

Answer #107: None. It's an open grave. You'll need dirt for a closed or covered grave.

Answer #108: A seesaw (see and saw).

Answer #109: February because it's the month that has the least number of days.

Answer #110: An alarm clock.

Answers 111-120

Answer #111: Time.

Answer #112: Charcoal.

Answer #113: The horizon.

Answer #114: The moon.

Answer #115: A shadow.

Answer #116: Jeremy.

Answer #117: He took the detour.

Answer #118: All of the fishes because the dead fishes - though floating on top of the water - are still in it.

Answer #119: All of their kids are girls so it's possible that half of them are girls.

Answer #120: 3 flowers and 4 bees.

Answers 121-130

Answer #121: This year because every year, New Year's day comes before Christmas day.

Answer #122: Sunshine.

Answer #123: The spare tire.

Answer #124: The two boys played against different opponents.

Answer #125: None. They don't drink milk.

Answer #126: Just one - it's the last brick that'll complete the building.

Answer #127: Just one - you!

Answer #128: Meow, meow!

Answer #129: Tell the king he'd like to die from old age.

Answer #130: The man was the keeper of a lighthouse and because he turned off the lights at night, boats crashed into the rocks or each other, leaving many of their passengers and crew dead.

Answers 131-140

Answer #131: Incorrectly is spelled as it should be spelled.

Answer #132: Their mother was on a boat when the twins were born, which was on a leap year. Mike was born a few minutes into March 1 and by the time mark was born, the boat crossed into a different time zone, which at that time was still February 28. So every leap year, when February has a 29th day, Mark's birthday is 2 days before Mike's.

Answer #133: Bread

Answer #134: The hungry lion attacking a tiger. Chances are high that they'll fatally wound each other, which means you have all the time in the world to escape both.

Answer #135: Jim and Janice were fish. When the train passed by in front of the house, its rumble was strong enough to topple the aquarium off the shelf and crash to the floor.

Answer #136: A bell.

Answer #137: The outside.

Answer #138: A postman

Answer #139: The right answer would be yes because if it had no holes, then how could you have worn it?

Answer #140: None, because all of them are copycats, which meant the other 19 followed the cat who jumped out of the truck.

Answers 141-150

Answer #141: Neither of them because the accountant happened to be the lawyer's sister.

Answer #142: From the pea-hen, she is the one laying the eggs.

Answer #143: There are two letter t's in the word "that".

Answer #144: None, because all the other 49 got scared and flew away.

Answer #145: The last kid to have a banana the basket that contained the last banana. Hence, there was one banana left in the basket.

Answer #146: 100 gold fishes were still left because gold fishes don't drown in water.

Answer #147: One is 50 cents and the other is a nickel. I didn't say both coins weren't nickels, only one. Hence, what are the two coins is a nickel.

Answer #148: 0-0, because that is always the score of any ball game before they start.

Answer #149: Boxing.

Answer #150: The two people were married and therefore, they weren't single people anymore.

Answers 151-160

Answer #151: Words.

Answer #152: I would love to swim in martian language.

Answer #153: 6 outs are needed because each team gets three outs.

Answer #154: A river.

Answer #155: No they weren't because all 3 doctors were women and hence, Michael's sisters.

Answer #156: The first store that they robbed was a clothing store and when they came out of it, they changed all of the clothes they were wearing. That's why they were completely changed when they went out of the first store that they robbed.

Answer #157: Neither of them because if they met, that means they were on the same location and therefore, same distance from Boston.

Answer #158: The people inside the car were a grandmother, a mother, and a daughter. A grandmother is also a mother that's why there were two mothers. The mother is also a daughter because she is the child of the grandmother and therefore, there were also two daughters in the car.

Answer #159: In the dictionary.

Answer #160: Just once because after that, you will be folding a much smaller piece of paper.

Answers 161-170

Answer #161: Leaves.

Answer #162: All of them have at least 28 days.

Answer #163: The letter e.

Answer #164: Because all the other days are week (weak) days.

Answer #165: A library because of the sheer number of books that tell stories it contains.

Answer #166: Your pride.

Answer #167: Salt.

Answer #168: Temperature.

Answer #169: Holes.

Answer #170: It's Christmas, eve!

Answers 171-180

Answer #171: Toys will be toys.

Answer #172: "Thanks Santa. I'll never part (my hair) with it!"

Answer #173: The split.

Answer #174: Fish and ships.

Answer #175: Grave-y.

Answer #176: I lava you!

Answer #177: A car tune (cartoon).

Answer #178: A fruit fly.

Answer #179: A normal person, because a normal person's right hand only contains five fingers.

Answer #180: Your dad!

Answers 181-190

Answer #181: A pine apple (pineapple).

Answer #182: It doesn't matter. Just make sure you listen carefully when it talks!

Answer #183: Spongebob smarty pants!

Answer #184: The letter d.

Answer #185: A toothbrush, a bed, and a chair. It doesn't have to be all in one you know.

Answer #186: Mooooon!

Answer #187: Stairs.

Answer #188: Tinsel-itis.

Answer #189: They become a milkshake.

Answer #190: They become hot dogs.

Answers 191-200

Answer #191: A yardstick.

Answer #192: A blood test.

Answer #193: The word ton, which, when reversed becomes not.

Answer #194: Wholesome.

Answer #195: The.

Answer #196: The letter u.

Answer #197: The farmer is minding his stock while the student is stocking his mind.

Answer #198: What is the first letter of the alphabet###the letter t of the word the.

Answer #199: A peli-can!

Answer #200: A hot air baboon.

Answers 201-210

Answer #201: A mushroom.

Answer #202: Running out of gas.

Answer #203: The other half of an apple.

Answer #204: The sea.

Answer #205: 194.

Answer #206: The outside part.

Answer #207: What time is it?

Answer #208: What happened to you when you died?

Answer #209: What word is spelled y, e, and s?

Answer #210: Almost.

Answers 211-220

Answer #211: Bacon.

Answer #212: The letter n.

Answer #213: A gun.

Answer #214: Post office. It's the place with the most letters (mail) inside.

Answer #215: The same as today.

Answer #216: Look away - I'm changing!

Answer #217: Santa Claus getting stuck in an elevator.

Answer #218: It has noel (no "l").

Answer #219: Roots.

Answer #220: A penguin rolling downhill.

Answers 221-230

Answer #221: A clock. You add 2 hours to 11:00 and you end up with 1:00.

Answer #222: In the dictionary.

Answer #223: A light switch.

Answer #224: Eating a watermelon because green means it's not yet ripe while red means it's ready for eating.

Answer #225: South because when you're traveling away from the North Pole, you're going south.

Answer #226: Underground, as all potatoes do.

Answer #227: The clock that doesn't work at all because it will tell the correct time twice a day, which is the time on which it is stuck. The other clock on the other hand after 720 days, at which point it had already lost 12 hours or 720 minutes.

Answer #228: 2 tons of cotton because the steel is only one ton.

Answer #229: Neither, because carrots are not color green.

Answer #230: Triangle A because a triangle with dimensions 700, 400, and 300 can never exist.

Answers 231-240

Answer #231: Santa paws.

Answer #232: It's the turkey because it's always stuffed.

Answer #233: A chess player.

Answer #234: Olaf - olaf the other reindeer, used to laugh and call him names.

Answer #235: The baby because he's a little bigger.

Answer #236: Fake money.

Answer #237: It's because 2017 (2,017) has 1 more dollar bill than 2016 (2,016) dollar bills.

Answer #238: Because it wasn't peeling well.

Answer #239: Hey bud (flower bud), when do you open?

Answer #240: Holes.

Answers 241-250

Answer #241: The blond because she had to ask for directions on the way down.

Answer #242: The bus driver was walking that time, not driving a bus.

Answer #243: It's a good batter.

Answer #244: It has to wear so many shoes.

Answer #245: It's because it was feeling crummy.

Answer #246: He wrote "whatever you're thinking" on paper, which is what he said he'd do.

Answer #247: The letter "e".

Answer #248: The letter "i".

Answer #249: A fence.

Answer #250: Water.

Answers 251-260

Answer #251: The ice. Breaking the ice means to relieve tension or get conversations going.

Answer #252: The letters "v" and "e".

Answer #253: The rain.

Answer #254: Nothing. Nothing's badder and bigger than the devil and god, respectively. Poor people have nothing and rich people can't have "nothing" because they have a lot of things. And eating nothing means going hungry and dying eventually.

Answer #255: To space.

Answer #256: Because bikes are 2-tired (too tired).

Answer #257: A bubble.

Answer #258: A lampshade.

Answer #259: It's because you can't arrest hurricanes.

Answer #260: Surname.

Answers 261-270

Answer #261: They live in different places. Eskimos live in the North Pole and penguins in the South Pole.
Answer #262: We are a team of game officials.

Answer #263: Wake up.

Answer #264: A palm tree because they look at people's palms (hands) to read their futures.

Answer #265: It wasn't raining.

Answer #266: If he marries off his son or daughter.

Answer #267: You have arms on your body, don't you?

Answer #268: With the paws (pause) button.

Answer #269: Use a key to the door.

Answer #270: When you're chewing gum in class, your teacher will say "spit it out!" But when you're chewing gum on a train, it will say "choo choo choo!" (chew, chew, chew)!

Answers 271-280

Answer #271: A riddle.

Answer #272: A dog, which is taller when sitting.

Answer #273: A human being.

Answer #274: A nose, which can be runny at times.

Answer #275: A highlighter.

Answer #276: A heart.

Answer #277: A peach.

Answer #278: A ring.

Answer #279: Ice.

Answer #280: A bat.

Answers 281-290

Answer #281: 1980 is a hotel room where I was born, not my birth year.

Answer #282: A carpet.

Answer #283: A room.

Answer #284: Jelly

Answer #285: A blue square.

Answer #286: The number 2. 2 added to 2 is 4 and 2 multiplied by 2 is also 4.

Answer #287: A snot-zi!

Answer #288: A doctopus.

Answer #289: What.

Answer #290: In a carpool.

Answers 291-300

Answer #291: Seaweed.

Answer #292: Open the window to let the bat out!

Answer #293: "c" and "y".

Answer #294: Jump from the door on the first floor of the building. You'll land safely outside the building.

Answer #295: A dead one.

Answer #296: In the middle.

Answer #297: Frostbite.

Answer #298: Nothing because it shuts up.

Answer #299: 50 cent (the rapper).

Answer #300: In the riverbank.

Answers 300-310

Answer #301: Just walk to it. The leash is much longer than the distance to the bone so there shouldn't be any problems getting the bone.

Answer #302: Every lunch time, it always goes back 4 (for) seconds.

Answer #303: The letter "o".

Answer #304: Your future.

Answer #305: None. You should get out immediately because your house is on fire!

Answer #306: Can't say - there's no answer!

Answer #307: A towel. The more it dries you, the wetter it becomes.

Answer #308: Nothing. You're just imagining it, remember?

Answer #309: A baseball team. It has 9 players with 2 legs each and they catch fly balls.

Answer #310: A liar.

Answers 311-320

Answer #311: A needle and thread.

Answer #312: An hourglass.

Answer #313: A horse with a person riding it.

Answer #314: A cow that is walking in reverse.

Answer #315: An echo.

Answer #316: A stapler.

Answer #317: Light.

Answer #318: A wedding ring.

Answer #319: A cherry.

Answer #320: A ton.

Answers 321-330

Answer #321: Parenthesis. It surrounds the world and galaxy (the world) (the galaxy).

Answer #322: A train.

Answer #323: A fox. Take away the letter "f" it becomes an ox!

Answer #324: It's because there's too many cheetahs (cheaters) there!

Answer #325: A frog in a blender.

Answer #326: Summer season. Because it's hot, so many people use lots of fans to cool themselves.

Answer #327: A rope or a chain.

Answer #328: A donut.

Answer #329: A camera. He gave it to someone random so that person can take his picture, after which that person returned it to James.

Answer #330: Jamie is blind and he's reading from a braille.

Answers 331-340

Answer #331: Jane was born on a leap year so by 2006, she has only celebrated 14 birthdays, compared to her son Darwin who has already celebrated 27 birthdays.

Answer #332: Fish. Since he sells fish by the pound, he has to weigh them.

Answer #333: Mercury.

Answer #334: A well.

Answer #335: Marge's dad is already dead.

Answer #336: She's wrong because if she's right, then it means her statement isn't a lie, which means not everything she tells you is a lie. If she's lying, then it means some of the things she'll tell you aren't lies.

Answer #337: Marv asked a question that had no answer such as "what is?"

Answer #338: Volcano.

Answer #339: Me!

Answer #340: My siblings were triplets.

Answers 341-350

Answer #341: Teeth.

Answer #342: Boooooo!

Answer #343: There were 3 of them: a knight (a night), a man, and a woman. If 3 of them hopped on a boat designed to accommodate 2 people only, it'll sink.

Answer #344: Because he nose (knows) a lot.

Answer #345: Because seven eight (ate) nine!

Answer #346: A key to the house.

Answer #347: The lone ranger. He always rides on his horse, silver.

Answer #348: The letter a, which starts the word awesomeness, ends the word comma, and is inside the word stomach.

Answer #349: The mother and son go first because they make a total weight of only 200 pounds. Once on the other side, the mother gets off and the son goes back for the father. Then, the father gets on the raft after the son gets off, and rows by himself to the other side. The father gets off, the mother gets on and goes back for the son on the other side of the river. Together, mother and son ride the raft to the other side, where the dad's already waiting.

Answer #350: Vege-tables!

Answers 351-360

Answer #351: 30 heads mean there were 30 foreheads.

Answer #352: Tonight (2,9), want (1) to (2) fight (5)!

Answer #353: It's trunk (like the trunk of a car or a big box).

Answer #354: They hit and destroyed each other.

Answer #355: Salt and pepper.

Answer #356: It's because they're all suckers!

Answer #357: Because it's the only way to take it...we can't chew it.

Answer #358: An equal.

Answer #359: A pork chop!

Answer #360: Smarties!

Answers 361-370

Answer #361: Finland.

Answer #362: The letter "e".

Answer #363: The word and.

Answer #364: A search.

Answer #365: They're the 3 blind mice because they have no eyes (letter i).

Answer #366: A blood hound.

Answer #367: The dictionary.

Answer #368: Properly.

Answer #369: The letter "t".

Answer #370: The river in a map.

Answers 371-380

Answer #371: The letter g.

Answer #372: Sdrawkcab, it's the word "spelled" backwards or in reverse.

Answer #373: Let someone throw it at you.

Answer #374: Too wise for me, too wise you are

Answer #375: Just put it on my bill (beak).

Answer #376: The ape-b-c's (abc's).

Answer #377: A candle.

Answer #378: A dog having puppies.

Answer #379: Language. It's the 3rd word of "the english language".

Answer #380: A feather. When it's on a bird, it flies. When it's off a bird, it just floats.

Answers 381-390

Answer #381: A game you never play.

Answer #382: A woman who wanted to put make up (face powder) on guns.

Answer #383: Because he had no body (nobody) to go with. He's a ghost, remember?

Answer #384: Because it saw a food to run after - a mouse!

Answer #385: To get to the other slide!

Answer #386: It's very hard to walk.

Answer #387: A newspaper.

Answer #388: The letter "e".

Answer #389: Your breath.

Answer #390: Microwave.

Answers 391-400

Answer #391: A remark.

Answer #392: Pastree (pastry).

Answer #393: The second coat, which is the logical coat to go "on the first" (on top of the first) coat.

Answer #394: Pull out the tub's stopper so water will drain from the tub.

Answer #395: A red bucket.

Answer #396: The outside. You don't find mugs with handles facing towards the inside of mugs, right?

Answer #397: One hour only because 10 pm is only an hour after 9 pm.

Answer #398: As old as you are. You're the pilot, remember?

Answer #399: Your car's name is Tuesday. You drove on it going to and from your parents' house within 5 days.

Answer #400: A clock.

Conclusion

Thanks for buying this book! I hope you and your kids had a fun and great time answering even more challenging riddles! And in case you haven't checked out the first 400 riddles in my previous book, I encourage you to check them out and get the first book Smart Riddles for Smart Kids. I'm sure you'll have even more fun! Until next time, all the best!

10819264R00074

Printed in Great Britain
by Amazon